PAST and PRESENT

No 45

Map of the area covered by this book, showing locations featured or referred to in the text.

BRITISH RAILWAYS

PAST and PRESENT

No 45

Sussex

Terry Gough

Past and Present

Past & Present Publishing Ltd

First published in 2004

British Library Cataloguing in Publication Data

A catalogue record for this book is available from the British Library.

ISBN 1 85895 239 5

Past & Present Publishing Ltd
The Trundle
Ringstead Road
Great Addington
Kettering
Northants NN14 4BW

Tel/Fax: 01536 330588
email: sales@nostalgiacollection.com
Website: www.nostalgiacollection.com

Printed and bound in Great Britain

All photographs were taken by the author unless otherwise credited, and all items of ephemera are from the author's collection.

HEATHFIELD: On 29 March 1961 BR Standard 4MT No 80146 enters the station on the 2.45pm train from Eastbourne to Tunbridge Wells West. This was a delightful station with a small goods yard to the left and a tunnel at the London end of the station behind the camera.

By the summer of 2003 all has been destroyed and it is difficult to appreciate that there was a railway here. Remnants of the platforms do exist but are out of sight, as are some of the houses in the background of the earlier view.

CONTENTS

BIBLIOGRAPHY

Gough, Terry *British Railways Past & Present No 46: Kent* (Past & Present Publishing, 2004) ISBN 1 85895 238 7
British Railways Past & Present Companion: The Bluebell Railway (Past & Present Publishing, 1998) ISBN 1 85895 129 1
British Railways Past & Present Companion: The Kent & East Sussex Railway (Past & Present Publishing, 1998) ISBN 1 85895 149 6
Rediscovering Railways: West Sussex (Past & Present Publishing, 2002) ISBN 1 85895 212 3

The Southern Railway Collection: Kent and Sussex (Silver Link Publishing, 2004) ISBN 1 85794 127 6
The Southern Railway Collection: Branch Lines Recalled (Silver Link Publishing, 1999) ISBN 1 85794 126 8
Kidner, R. W. *Southern Railway Halts* (Oakwood Press, 1985) ISBN 0 85361 321 4
Morrison, Brian and Beer, Brian *British Railways Past & Present No 20: Kent and East Sussex* (Silver Link Publishing, 1994) ISBN 1 85895 044 9

EASTBOURNE: On 13 April 1962 a welcome change from the frequent arrival and departure of electric units was the hourly steam-operated service to and from Tunbridge Wells. The 9.41am from Tunbridge Wells West enters Eastbourne behind Standard 4MT No 80082.

On 1 August 1987 Class 421 (4-CIG) No 1110 leaves as the 14.06 Ore to Brighton service. On the right Class 415 (4-EPB) No 5442 is in use as a mail train.

INTRODUCTION

This book covers the two counties of East and West Sussex. Railway development was undertaken mainly by the London, Brighton & South Coast Railway (LBSCR), except in the area bordered by Kent, for which the South Eastern & Chatham Railway (SECR) was mostly responsible. Both became part of the Southern Railway in 1923 and the Southern Region of British Railways in 1948. The railways have been transformed out of all recognition since the early days, resulting in both success and failure.

The success stems mainly from the fact that the former LBSCR main lines were electrified in the 1930s, and from the incredible population growth along the coast and at many of the inland towns served by the railways. A more recent success has been the introduction of through services from Brighton to Bedford and Luton, under the name 'Thameslink'. On the former SECR main line from London to Hastings, diesel multiple units (DMUs) were introduced as early as 1957, to be displaced by electric multiple units (EMUs) in 1986.

Failure lies in the inability to anticipate the rapid expansion of smaller towns served by secondary routes, many of which have lost their rail services. A comparison of the railway map of early BR days and the present day shows the virtual extinction of lesser lines. For example, there are no longer trains from Horsham to either Guildford or Brighton, there is no direct link from East Grinstead to Three Bridges, and there are no railways from Eastbourne and Brighton to Tunbridge Wells. In some instances, housing estates have been built on the former station sites.

The London to Brighton via Oxted and East Grinstead line has had mixed fortunes. It was electrified in 1987 as far as East Grinstead and enjoys a frequent service to London throughout the day. South of East Grinstead the line is closed as far as Kingscote, but is operated by the Bluebell Railway from there to Sheffield Park. Between Sheffield Park and Lewes the railway has been abandoned.

One of the poorest decisions regarding rail services relates to Uckfield on the Oxted and Tunbridge Wells to Brighton line. In addition to regular services throughout the day, there were morning and evening through trains to and from London. The line now terminates at Uckfield with an hourly shuttle service to Oxted, although a small number of London trains have been retained. Proposals to re-open the line on to Lewes are periodically considered, but as the years pass this is becoming increasingly unlikely.

Uckfield station was on the west side of the level crossing that carries the A22 main road. The building of a bypass, while reducing traffic through the town, has dissected the abandoned line. It was, however, still deemed necessary to relocate the station to the east (London) side of the road, thereby further reducing the possibility of re-instating the line to Lewes. The new station consists of a single platform, with no run-round facilities. Plans to electrify the Uckfield line from Oxted (Hurst Green Junction) have been abandoned. However, there is a possibility of one day restoring services between Tunbridge Wells and Eridge under the auspices of the Spa Valley Railway, which at present operates as a heritage line as far as Groombridge; such a service could connect with Uckfield line trains.

Further east, part of the Kent & East Sussex Railway falls within the area covered by this book, but the section from Robertsbridge to Bodiam remains closed. From Bodiam across the county boundary into Kent is a heritage railway service. The line from Hastings to Rye and Ashford is still open and operated by DMUs, plans to electrify this line having been abandoned.

Locomotives and rolling-stock have, of course, also changed over the decades, but steam trains still operate on the Bluebell Railway, Spa Valley Railway and Kent & East Sussex

Railway. These feature engines from the pre-Southern Railway era, and others built more recently, including engines representing classes used on those lines in the past as well as some 'foreign' examples. On the national network, all the Southern Railway EMUs have long gone, and even their successors built in BR days are virtually life-expired. Most of the BR Mark I 'slam door' stock was due to be withdrawn by the end of 2004. At the time of writing, newly built air-conditioned EMUs were being introduced. Also at the time of writing new DMUs had just started work on the Uckfield and Hastings to Ashford lines, which will result in withdrawal of the early BR units known as 'Thumpers'. Other modern DMUs can be seen on services from Reading to Brighton. An interesting innovation in 1988 was the introduction of dual-voltage EMUs, built for the Thameslink services. These collect power from the third rail south of the River Thames and from overhead wires north of the river.

Locomotive-hauled trains have always been in the minority since the SR electrification programme. BR-built dual-power electro-diesels and ordinary diesel locomotives were seen across the region until the virtual demise of freight trains. The only regular present-day diesel-hauled trains are passenger services from Cardiff. Cross-country trains, formerly operated by diesel locomotives, are now formed of 'Voyager' DMUs.

The days of BR Southern Region and Network South East (NSE) are over, although some trains to this day retain NSE livery. Following privatisation, the major Train Operating Company providing services in Sussex was Connex, but this company lost its franchise in August 2001. Services were then provided by South Central, which changed its name to Southern in May 2004. Connex South Eastern provided services on the London to Hastings main line, but from November 2003 this changed to South Eastern Trains. Thameslink Rail runs services from north of the River Thames. Services from Surrey and Hampshire are operated by South West Trains and cross-country services by Virgin Trains. Services from South Wales were operated until 2001 by Wales & West and currently by Wessex Trains. All this, together with the Bluebell Railway, Kent & East Sussex Railway, the Lavender Line and Spa Valley Railway, makes the railways of Sussex both interesting and colourful.

Terry Gough, Sherborne

ACKNOWLEDGEMENTS

I thank the various photographers who have kindly loaned me material for this book. British Railways provided a lineside pass for the 'past' views, while the majority of 'present' views are accessible to the public. For those locations on private land, I am grateful for permission to enter. Colin Pattle and Dick Ware are thanked for providing information on current practice. I am also grateful to my wife for spending part of a short holiday in Sussex hunting for abandoned stations.

Brighton toward Havant

BRIGHTON (1): Brighton-Plymouth trains were usually worked by 'West Country' Class locomotives until the end of steam. Fewer through trains were provided when diesels took over, and one such train was the 11.12 to Paignton, which, on 1 August 1987, was worked as usual by a Class 33, in this instance No 33204.

There is still a through train to Plymouth, which runs on Sundays only and is formed of a Class 159 DMU. There is also one locomotive-hauled train out of Brighton, running on Fridays only and top-and-tailed by Class 31s. This is the 17.00 service to Cardiff Central, worked on 4 April 2003 by Nos 31468 *Hydra* and 31602 *Chimaera*. On the left is newly introduced Class 375 No 375312 forming the 16.26 Seaford to Littlehampton service.

BRIGHTON (2): A train from Horsham arrives at Brighton on 8 June 1962 with an LMSR-designed 4MT and Maunsell coaches. To the right is the motive power depot, with BR Standard 4MTs and a 'West Country' 'Pacific'.

On 7 March 2003 the 12.00 Wessex Trains service from Cardiff Central, formed of Class 158 No 158864, enters the station. Class 421 (4-CIG) No 1855 is berthed on the left.

BRIGHTON SHED is seen on 8 June 1962, with Class 'E4' No 32503 in the foreground. This was a very interesting depot, with an allocation of approximately 70 locomotives from LBSCR 'Terriers' to Bulleid 'Pacifics'. The site of the shed is still used for railway purposes today, including a maintenance depot.

BRIGHTON (3): Leaving the station beneath the magnificent overall roof on 1 August 1987 is Class 73 No 73101 *The Royal Alex*, which had brought in the empty stock for a Paignton train.

A return visit on 4 April 2003 found a Class 319 on a Bedford train and a Mark I EMU entering the platform on a train from Littlehampton.

HOLLAND ROAD HALT was the first station out of Brighton in the direction of Havant. Opened in 1905, it closed in 1956. Two months prior to closure two Class 2-NOL units stop with a Brighton to West Worthing service.

On a wet day in March 2003 South West Trains Class 170 No 170303 passes the site of the halt forming the 10.00 Brighton to Reading service. The curvature of the line is accentuated by the use of a telephoto lens. In the background, the square-shaped building on the right still stands, but has been modified. *Edwin Wilmshurst/TG*

HOVE (1): Class 'K' No 32353 approaches Hove from the east with a special train on the evening of 7 October 1962. These engine were more commonly seen on freight trains throughout the Central Section of the SR.

Old and new cross at Hove on 9 March 2003. Class 375 No 375314 approaches forming the 13.26 Seaford to Littlehampton service, while on the left Class 421 (4-CIG) No 1834 heads for Brighton as the 14.14 from Littlehampton.

14

HOVE (2): On 1 August 1987 there is plenty of activity at Hove. On the far left Class 73 No 73132 arrives in the yard on an engineers' train, while platforms 1 and 3 are both occupied by Class 421s (4-CIG), Nos 1801 and 1802 respectively. The former is the 15.51 service from Brighton to Littlehampton, and the latter the 16.04 Brighton to West Worthing.

There are still occasional locomotive-hauled trains at Hove, the Friday-only Brighton to Cardiff train and VSOE excursions from Victoria. On 7 March 2003 the VSOE train is hauled by Class 47 No 47784 as it returns to London via the Coast Line.

ALDRINGTON HALT: A Sentinel railcar was used on the Dyke branch between 1933 and 1935, and is seen at Aldrington Halt en route to Brighton on 11 October 1933. The halt opened as Dyke Junction in 1905 and was renamed in 1932.

Nothing more interesting than a train of BR Mark I coaches of Class 421 (4-CIG) No 1902 was at Aldrington on 4 April 2003, forming the 12.14 Littlehampton to Seaford service. *H. C. Casserley/TG*

GOLF CLUB HALT: The junction for the branch to The Dyke, opened in 1887 and closed on the last day of 1938, was just west of Aldrington Halt. The branch had two intermediate stations: this is Golf Club Halt, opened as a private facility in 1891, and photographed on 5 September 1955. The other halt, at Rowan, did not open until 1933.

The golf course is still in use and the site of the halt recognisable. The course of the line in this area is also easy to see, but further south toward Aldrington much has been obliterated by housing and other developments.

THE DYKE: This is the terminus in LBSCR days with Class 'E3' No 168 *Southborough* arriving from Brighton. The site is now part of a farm, but there are several clear indications that there was once a railway here. The second view is of approximately the same location in July 1999. *John Stretton collection/TG*

PORTSLADE & WEST HOVE: The Lancing Works train, known as the 'Lancing Belle', was steam-worked and usually double-headed by LBSCR tank engines, as here on 5 June 1962, when the afternoon return train to Brighton was worked by Class 'E4' Nos 32503 and 32468, seen approaching Portslade & West Hove.

The suffix 'West Hove' was added in 1927 and dropped in the late 1970s. On 4 April 2003 state-of-the-art Class 375 No 375318 enters Portslade as the 11.12 Portsmouth Harbour to Brighton service. *Edwin Wilmshurst/TG*

LANCING CARRIAGE WORKS: This general view of the carriage shop yard was taken on 14 March 1965, the year in which the works closed. The boiler house and smith shop are on the far right.

The area occupied by the Carriage Works is now an industrial estate, consisting mostly of purpose-built buildings. However, the carriage shop was not demolished and is currently used as a furniture factory. The 'past' view can no longer be photographed from the same position because of the proximity of new buildings on what was the yard. However, this is a side view across the end of the building on 4 April 2003. *Edwin Wilmshurst/TG*

EAST WORTHING HALT: Worthing has three stations, the first from the Brighton direction being East Worthing Halt, seen here on 20 August 1966 and 4 April 2003. On the latter date, a welcome change from EMUs is this South West Trains Class 159 No 159019 forming the 09.25 Basingstoke to Brighton service. Most of these services are operated by EMUs (usually Class 423s), and it is normally only trains to and from Reading that are formed of DMUs, the Basingstoke-Reading line not being electrified. *C. L. Caddy/TG*

WORTHING CENTRAL: Class 2-BIL EMUs cross at Worthing Central on 5 September 1970. On the right is No 2036 forming a Littlehampton to Brighton train, while on the left, travelling away from Brighton, is unit No 2103.

On 5 March 2004 the 12.00 Cardiff Central to Brighton train is headed by Class 31 No 31452 *Minotaur*. On the return working the train was diverted to Portsmouth Harbour, where the service was terminated; the stock was then used for the 18.24 Portsmouth Harbour to Cardiff Central to replace a failed DMU. *J. H. Aston/TG*

WEST WORTHING is seen looking towards Brighton on 21 March 1970. Some 30 years later, on 28 July 1999, the canopies have been removed on both platforms, and in the platform is Class 421 (3-COP) No 1410 forming the 11.22 service from here to Brighton. Three-coach formations were very unusual for BR Mark I EMUs: there were only 11 such units, formed from 4-CIGs in 1997/8 specifically for the Brighton-Portsmouth services. *Edwin Wilmshurst/TG*

FORD: Only 16 years ago, but certainly 'past', Class 33 No 33029 takes an infrastructure train through Ford on 21 May 1988 on its way to Chichester Yard. To the right is the defunct bay for the shuttle service to Littlehampton.

The Friday-only locomotive-hauled 17.00 Brighton to Cardiff Central train gives a brief and welcome return to a previous era. On 13 June 2003 Class 31 No 31468 *Hydra* heads the train through Ford. On the rear is No 31602 *Chimaera*.

BARNHAM: Electro-diesel Class 73 No 73124 takes an Eastleigh to St Leonards freight train through Barnham on 21 August 1985. The converted covered carriage truck contains a refurbished power unit for a Hastings DMU.

On 4 April 2003 Class 375 No 375332, forming the 09.12 Portsmouth Harbour to Brighton service, passes the signal box at the west end of the station, which is still in use. The semaphore signals have, however, been replaced by colour lights. *Roger Marsh/TG*

BOGNOR REGIS is the terminus of a branch from Branham, and this pre-Grouping photograph shows Class 'D1' No 288 on a typical LBSCR local train. It is amazing how little the station has changed over about 80 years. Apart from electrification and the replacement of canopies, there are no major differences. The EMU is Class 421 (4-CIG) No 1737 in unmarked white livery. *Lens of Sutton/TG*

CHICHESTER: On 25 May 1988 two Class 33s were active in Chichester Yard. This is No 33020 running light to Brighton after completing some shunting. On the right is the 12.25 Brighton to Portsmouth Harbour slow train formed of Class 423 (4-VEP) No 3090.

Two diesel locomotives appeared at Chichester on the afternoon of 13 June 2003 on the 12.00 Cardiff Central to Brighton train. On the rear was Class 31 No 31486 *Hydra*, and the train was hauled by No 31602 *Chimaera*. On the right is Class 411 (4-CEP) No 1539 forming the 14.00 South West Trains service from Brighton to Basingstoke.

SOUTHBOURNE HALT is seen first in 1970, complete with traditional signal box and crossing gates. A return visit about 30 years later found that the box was still in use, although the gates had been replaced. Class 423 (4-VEP) No 3518 forms a Portsmouth Harbour to Brighton slow train.

Lines around Midhurst

MIDHURST station closed to passenger services on 5 February 1955, but occasional special passenger trains continued to run. One such was the 'West Sussex Downsman', a ramblers' excursion from London on 8 June 1958, hauled by Class 'Q' No 30549. The station area has since been redeveloped and is occupied by houses, as can be seen in the present-day view.

SOUTHERN RAILWAY.
Issued subject to the Bye-laws, Regulations &
Conditions in the Company's Bills and Notices.
Available on DAY of issue ONLY.

Midhurst to
LONDON BRIDGE or VICTORIA
Via Pulborough

THIRD CLASS

Issued in exchange for Period Return Ticket
issued by London Coastal Coaches Limited or
Southdown Motor Services Limited upon
payment of the supplementary charge of 7/6
NOT TRANSFERABLE.

SELHAM: The Midhurst-Pulborough line and most of the stations were retained long after withdrawal of passenger services, and special passenger trains would occasionally visit the line. This is Selham station on 24 June 1962.

The track has since been removed, but Selham station still stands and at the time of this second visit 30 years later it was in use as a private house.

Mid-Sussex line

LITTLEHAMPTON: This 1970 view shows the island platform, goods shed and yard. The coach is in Departmental use as a mobile office and numbered DS70078; a Maunsell Brake 3rd, it was built for the Eastern Section of the SR in 1924 and numbered 3569.

In the more recent view, the coach has gone but the goods shed still stands. Even more surprising is the continued use of semaphore signals.

ARUNDEL: The 9.56am train from Victoria to Portsmouth passes through Arundel on 10 October 1932 behind Class 'I3' No B30.

There are no regular locomotive-hauled trains on this line today, but on 3 July 2003 a track-recording train top-and-tailed by two Class 47s, Nos 47778 *Irresistible* and 47792 *Saint Cuthbert*, pass through Arundel. A second canopy has been added to the down platform and a footbridge connects the two platforms. *H. C. Casserley/TG*

BILLINGSHURST station is conveniently situated in the town, and this is the country end of the station, from which it can be seen that little has changed between 1970 and 1999. The station opened in 1859, but the line only went as far as Petworth. The line south to Ford was opened in 1863 from Hardham Junction, and Petworth became part of the Midhurst branch (see page 29). The Mid Sussex line was electrified in 1938.

CHRIST'S HOSPITAL: This unusual formation is the result of combining push-pull passenger stock with a van not so fitted. Class 'M7' No 30052 is propelling coaches out of Christ's Hospital towards Brighton as the 10.19am service from Horsham on 24 March 1960. Bay platforms are on the left and beyond them is the coal yard. Separate platforms (behind the camera) were provided for the Guildford trains.

The grandeur of Christ's Hospital has been destroyed and it now has a simple up and down platform layout. The island platforms for school specials have gone and the Guildford platforms have been partly removed. On 24 April 2003 Class 375 No 375108 rushes through the station on a crew training run from Horsham.

HORSHAM: Approaching the station, its final destination, push-pull set No 736 is propelled by Class 'M7' No 30047 as the 10.08am train from Brighton on 8 June 1958.

Class 423 No 3917 forms the 09.08 service to Victoria on 4 April 2003, incorrectly showing headcode 16. This is one of 19 units of Class VEP converted for South London Metro services and reclassified 4-VOP. New colour light signals are in the process of being installed.

CRAWLEY station is seen looking east on 6 July 1968, three weeks before closure. There was a level crossing at the Horsham end of the station, behind the photographer.

A new station was built further away from the level crossing towards Three Bridges, and this opened on the day the old station closed. The old platforms still exist and can be seen in the photograph taken on 24 April 2003. The present-day station is in the distance. *Edwin Wilmshurst/TG*

THREE BRIDGES SHED had an allocation of about 30 locomotives, including several of Class 'K'; on 7 October 1962 No 32344 is seen in the shed yard.

Although the motive power depot has gone, the site is used by a railway maintenance company and was photographed again on 24 April 2003.

Brighton to Horsham

BRAMBER: The Horsham line left the coast line just west of Shoreham-by-Sea, and the first station was Bramber, seen here on 7 September 1963 with Horsham and Brighton trains crossing. By this time the pre-Grouping rolling-stock, mostly push-pull-operated, and the associated locomotives had been replaced by modern corridor stock and post-Nationalisation motive power. The down train consists of a Brighton-built Stanier 4MT and Bulleid set No 89. The station has since been totally obliterated by a roundabout and approach road. *J. H. Aston/TG*

RUDGWICK: Trains on the Horsham-Guildford line were worked by pre-Grouping locomotives for most of the route's existence. On 24 March 1961 Class 'E4' No 32475 with set No 600 is seen at Rudgwick forming the 9.30am train from Horsham. Today the station has gone and the trackbed is part of a long-distance footpath known as the Downs Link, which also uses much of the Horsham to Brighton line trackbed.

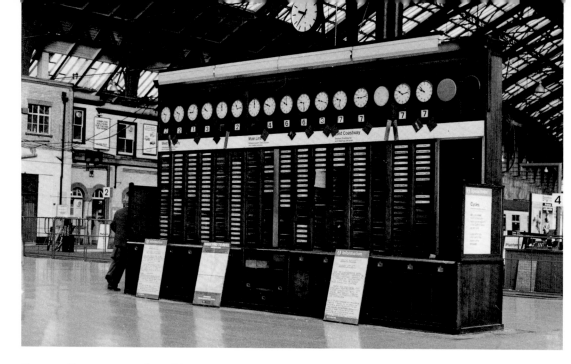

London main line from Brighton

BRIGHTON (4): The station boasted a traditional SR indicator board, as found at other major termini, including both Victoria and Waterloo.

The replacement indicator board has been positioned closer to the platform barriers. Despite this, the concourse is more cramped as several shops now trade here. This is the afternoon rush hour with commuters mingling with holidaymakers during Easter 2003. Note the attractive 'gas lamp'-style lighting. *Edwin Wilmshurst/TG*

BRIGHTON (5): 'Brighton Belle' unit No 3053, in its final BR livery, waits to leave for Victoria in 1970. There were three of these five-coach units, all built in 1932 and painted in Pullman livery. They were withdrawn in 1972, but all the coaches are still in existence, two forming part of the VSOE Pullman train.

The 'Brighton Belle' is no more, but there are other interesting trains to be seen. On 28 July 1999 the 14.18 Virgin Trains service to Preston leaves behind Class 47 No 47854 *Women's Royal Voluntary Service*. On the right is Class 319 No 319438 forming the 14.29 Thameslink service to Bedford.

BRIGHTON (6): Celebrating 150 years of the Brighton line on 21 September 1991 is the 'Brighton Belle' hauled by Class 73 electro-diesel No 73101 *Brighton Evening Argus* in Pullman livery, approaching the terminus.

A recently introduced Virgin Trains 'Voyager' forms the 08.53 service from Manchester Piccadilly to Brighton on 4 April 2003. It does not form the afternoon return trip, as it arrives in Brighton about an hour after the train to Manchester has left. In the sidings is newly delivered Class 375 EMU No 375333.

PRESTON PARK: An up freight train from Hove passes Preston Park behind Class 'K' No 32350 on 22 April 1961. The up and down main lines are to the left.

The track on the extreme right has become a footpath for permanent way gangs, and the up platform canopy and waiting room have been replaced. This is Preston Park on 4 April 2003.

BURGESS HILL: SR 4-LAV EMU No 2947 stands at Burgess Hill with a Victoria to Brighton via Redhill slow train on 19 September 1966. These units were built specifically for the semi-fast services on the Brighton line.

On 28 July 1999 Class 319 No 319216 forms the 14.32 Connex service from Victoria to Brighton. This is one of seven units refurbished specifically as Victoria to Brighton expresses and was originally numbered 319016. They are expected to be returned to Thameslink in September 2004. *J. H. Aston/TG*

Brighton to East Grinstead

BRIGHTON (7): Although the main and coast lines had been electrified for many years, there was still plenty of steam activity at Brighton in the early 1960s. This is the 7.55pm to Tonbridge, pulling out of the far platform (No 10) on the eastern side of the station on 8 June 1962. The engine is Class 'N' No 31865.

A visit on 1 August 1987 found that the track had been removed from platforms 9 and 10. Diesel shunter Class 09 No 09007 stands in platform 8.

Something altogether more grand was using platform 8 on 4 April 2003, with Virgin Trains Class 220 No 220010 *Ribble Voyager* forming the 13.18 service to Manchester Piccadilly. Until summer 2003 there was also a morning train to Manchester. During that year the 13.18 was withdrawn, but in 2004 it was re-instated, but there is no longer a morning train.

FALMER: Class 'N' No 31401 takes the Brighton breakdown train through Falmer to rescue a derailed train at Tunbridge Wells on the evening of 8 June 1962.

A visit to Falmer on 9 March 2003 proved difficult. There were no trains all day between Brighton and Lewes due to engineering works, to which the person on the track is contributing! The substitute bus service, despite claims, did not serve Falmer station in the eastbound direction and the weather was dreadful. Even worse, there were no notices at Falmer or Moulscomb advising passengers of the arrangements and the helplines had been switched off.

LEWES (1): This early post-Grouping photograph shows a train of SECR stock at Lewes on a Brighton to Tonbridge train. The engine is a Class 'O1' and it is hauling a 'birdcage' set. The station is in the vee of the junction between the lines from Brighton and London via Haywards Heath.

The line used by the 'past' train has been removed and the trackbed brought up to platform level. The second photograph, taken in August 1988, shows Class 416 (2-EPB) No 6303 on a parcels train to Brighton. *Lens of Sutton/TG*

BARCOMBE was a small station by LBSCR standards, and saw very little passenger traffic in latter days. It never re-opened after the rail strike of 1955 and the subsequent legal challenge over the closure, despite services being restored on the line for a short while. Here Class 4MT No 80151 takes a single coach from Lewes to East Grinstead through Barcombe in 1957 after the re-instatement of services. The goods yard was to the left behind the photographer.

The station house is a private residence and all that remains of the goods yard is one wooden gate-post. The station house is beyond the trees. *M. Esau/TG*

NEWICK & CHAILEY, on 30 May 1955, is deserted because of a rail strike. The station closed on 13 June of the same year during the strike, but was re-opened in August 1956, to close for ever in March 1958.

Nothing remains of the station and the site is occupied by houses, but there is evidence of the trackbed looking north from the site of the road overbridge immediately to the north of the station. This is the view looking south from the road bridge into the station site in March 1996.

London Brighton & South Coast Railway.

Hastings to

Newick & Chailey

SHEFFIELD PARK: On 31 August 1954 Class 4MT No 42104 arrives at Sheffield Park on the 12.03pm train from Victoria to Brighton.
    No one could have predicted in the 1950s how Sheffield Park would develop, and this 1996 view gives a sample of what has been achieved since preservation by the Bluebell Railway. *J. H. Aston/TG*

WEST HOATHLY: The track at West Hoathly was removed in 1964 using North London Railway engine No 2650 on the demolition train. Subsequently the station did not fare as well as other stations on the surviving part of the line, the station buildings being demolished in 1967. The second view shows all that remained in April 1992. There are, however, plans to build a new station. *Edwin Wilmshurst/TG*

KINGSCOTE: Before the first closure there were through trains between Brighton and London, and one such is leaving Kingscote in early 1955 behind Class 'K' No 32344.

Kingscote was the other station on the line that was not re-opened following the re-instatement of services by BR. However, the main station building here was not demolished, although the down side was destroyed and track removed. This February 1996 photograph shows that much has been rebuilt and trains are again using the station, which re-opened in April 1994. Class '4500' No 4561 is running round the train it has brought from Horsted Keynes. *P. Hay/TG*

EAST GRINSTEAD LOW LEVEL: On the last day of services to Lewes, 16 March 1958, 4MT No 80011 is ready to leave with the 10.38am departure from the Low Level station.

East Grinstead became a terminus for trains from Oxted and London, and following the end of steam these trains were worked by DMUs. On 1 May 1986 Class 205 (3H) No 1120 arrives with the 07.44 service from London Bridge.

The line was subsequently electrified, and DMUs were not seen again until 2003, when new Class 170s were under test prior to introduction on the Uckfield line. On 4 March 2004 recently formed unit No 3813 of Class 423 (4-VEP) leads the 08.25 service from London Bridge into the station.

Seaford to Horsted Keynes

SEAFORD: Class 'E4' No 32479 was photographed in Seaford yard on the occasion of a special passenger working on 7 October 1962.

Seaford remains open for passenger traffic, but the goods yard is occupied by houses, which block the view of the approach road to the bridge over the railway. Only one face of the station's island platform is in use, as seen on 10 April 2003.

NEWHAVEN TOWN: Another Class 'E4' on the Seaford branch, this time No 32504 with BR standard and SR brake-vans, is waiting to reverse on to the down line at Newhaven Town on 22 April 1961. The Harbour station is just round the corner out of sight, and Newhaven running shed is to the right, also out of view.

Class 375 units were introduced on Seaford services in the spring of 2003, and No 375322 effectively blocks the view ahead as it leaves Newhaven Town on 8 April forming the 13.14 service from Littlehampton to Seaford.

NEWHAVEN SHED was a sub-shed of Brighton, and housed Class 'A1Xs' for shunting on the harbour lines. On 22 April 1961 No 32670 is being coaled outside the shed. The shed closed in September 1963, but still exists today, and is used by an engineering company.

LEWES (2): This is the other arm of the vee of Lewes station (see page 53), accommodating trains from the main line from London via Haywards Heath. On 23 October 1934 a London Bridge to Ore train arrives at Lewes behind Class 'D' No 1748.

Several major changes have taken place in the ensuing years, the most obvious being electrification. The far side of the bay platform is a car park, the road overbridge has been rebuilt, the signal box relocated, and the crossover removed. On 13 March 1996 Class 422 (4-BIG) No 2206 forms the 09.50 Victoria to Eastbourne service via the Quarry Line. *H. C. Casserley/TG*

PLUMPTON is seen on 3 March 1934, with LBSCR Class 'L' No 2333 *Remembrance* on the 2.14pm Seaford to Haywards Heath train. A racecourse is adjacent to the railway, with direct access from the station.

A visit on 10 April 2003 found that much of Plumpton's character has been retained: the signal box and even the traditional level crossing gates are still in use. The main station building is in good order and the up-side waiting shelter is original. A three-coach unit of Class 421 (3-COP), No 1410, stops at Plumpton at 16.44 forming the 15.47 service from Victoria, which splits at Haywards Heath, the front portion for Eastbourne and Hastings and the rear portion for Littlehampton and Portsmouth Harbour. Plumpton has a sparse service much of the day, with only one train between the 09.44 and the 15.44. *H. C. Casserley/TG*

WIVELSFIELD is seen looking towards Brighton on 24 April 1937, four years after electrification. The railway is on an embankment and booking facilities, on the down side, are at street level.

Most of the original structure is still in place, although the platforms have been lengthened at the London end, giving ready access to the exact location for the present-day equivalent shot. On 4 April 2003 Class 319 No 319426 forms the 12.57 service from Bedford to Brighton. *H. C. Casserley/TG*

HAYWARDS HEATH is in the background of this 12 September 1969 view. Redundant coaches were often used as offices, and seen here is Maunsell Brake 3rd coach No DS70180. In the station is an SR 4-COR unit forming a Victoria to Brighton train.

The former goods yard is now a car park, and all EMUs were built post-Nationalisation, typified by this Class 319 on a Brighton-bound train on 28 March 1996. The buildings on the right of the 'past' view' have been demolished, but the taller building behind still stands.

ARDINGLY was the only station on the line connecting the London-Brighton main line with the alternative route via East Grinstead, and enjoyed an hourly service of electric trains between Seaford and Horsted Keynes on Mondays to Saturdays. On 21 October 1962 Class 2-HAL No 2657 stops briefly on it way to Horsted Keynes. Beyond the footbridge is a road overbridge.

The station closed to passengers the following year and the platforms were demolished. The line was slewed a little to the left and a stone depot built. The depot is served by a daily train, and here Class 59 No 59103 *Village of Mells* backs its wagons into the depot. The road overbridge is hidden by the depot equipment.

HORSTED KEYNES station was built to main-line proportions with five platforms, one of which was used as the terminus for the electrified branch from Haywards Heath. On 11 May 1958 the 10.25am arrival from Seaford is being worked by two 2-NOL units, Nos 1844 and 1821. Much has happened at Horsted Keynes since BR withdrew services from both the East Grinstead to Lewes line and the Haywards Heath line. Rolling-stock of the Bluebell Railway confirms that the station is again open for passengers, as seen on 11 April 1992.

71

Lewes to Groombridge

BARCOMBE MILLS was an attractive station, as seen in this 1970 photograph, looking towards Uckfield.

At the time of a second visit, on 24 October 1987, the railway was in the process of being demolished, while a third visit, on 1 July 2003, was a much happier occasion, as the station is now in private hands and the owners have painstakingly restored much of which was destroyed, with a little licence to suit their own particular requirements.

London Brighton & South Coast Railway.

Rotherfield to

Barcombe Mills

73

ISFIELD: This portrait of Isfield station shows the up platform in 1970, one year after closure. The station is in surprisingly good order, with no weeds on the trackbed, and the station hardware, such as nameboards, still in place.

The station subsequently passed into private ownership and now forms the headquarters of the Lavender Line. This is the view from the level crossing on 1 July 2003, looking in the same direction. The station is open to visitors most Sundays throughout the year and on summer Saturdays.

UCKFIELD (1): Class 'K' No 32339 shunts at Uckfield while 4MT No 80147 pulls out of the station on the 1.10pm train from Tonbridge to Brighton on 27 March 1961.

The line as far as Uckfield has been kept open, but there have been many changes. DMUs took over from steam trains and on 24 October 1987 Class 205 No 205009 and 205002 form the 13.42 service to Oxted.

The station was subsequently relocated on the Oxted and London side of the main road level crossing and the original station buildings have been demolished. If it is redeveloped, it is likely to mean the end of proposals to rebuild the line to Lewes. This is the desolate view on 5 March 2004, although both platforms, including lamp standards and track, are still in place.

UCKFIELD (2): The station is viewed from the Oxted side of the level crossing on 5 April 1986. In the up platform is Class 207 (3D) No 1316 forming the 15.35 service to London Bridge.

The new station is a scruffy single-platform affair and presents a poor image to passengers. It is hard to believe that this is the same place, but immediately beyond the rear of the train is the site of the level crossing and old station. Class 205 No 205033 has just arrived with the 12.04 service from Oxted on 5 April 2002. Despite the 'Coach Connex' sign on the platform, there was no connecting bus service to Lewes.

BUXTED is a small and well-kept station, seen here looking towards Uckfield in 1970. Since that date the up platform has been isolated by the removal of the track, and all trains use the old down line, but the booking office and waiting room are beautifully maintained by enthusiastic staff. On 5 April 2002 Class 205 No 205012 approaches the station forming the 15.00 Uckfield to Oxted service. Although the footbridge has gone it was not scrapped, but in 1990 was reassembled at Templecombe on the Waterloo to Exeter main line.

CROWBOROUGH & JARVIS BROOK was named Rotherfield until a station of that name was opened on the Eastbourne-Groombridge line, when it became Crowborough, then, in 1897, Crowborough & Jarvis Brook, reverting to Crowborough in the late 1970s. Class 'U1' No 31892 is seen at Crowborough on the 3.10pm train from Tonbridge to Brighton on 27 March 1961. In the other platform is the 2.56pm service from Brighton to Tonbridge.

Crowborough is another well-maintained station with excellent booking facilities. Here the double track has been retained. On 4 April 2002 Class 205 (3H) No 205001 forms the 12.00 service from Uckfield to East Croydon. The goods yard and shed, out of sight behind the camera, are used by a builders' merchant.

ERIDGE (1) was photographed on a wet morning in March 1961. In the loop is 4MT No 80017 on the 9.45am Eastbourne to Tonbridge service, and in the centre is Class 'U1' No 31906 on the 9.55am Brighton to Victoria train.

Although Eridge lost its services to Eastbourne and Tonbridge, it clung on to all its platforms for several years, as seen in this 1 May 1986 view.

ERIDGE (2): On 1 May 1986 Class 205 (3H) No 1123 forms the 12.09 service from Tonbridge, which terminated here. Although the down loop (extreme left) is blocked at the southern end, serving as a footway into the car park, all other lines are in use. On the extreme right sister unit No 1118 is in use in a film set.

A visit on a dismal afternoon in early December 2003 found the station in a decrepit state, with major repairs long overdue. One welcome aspect was the lack of damage by vandals. In contrast to the station, Class 170 No 170723 enters the station from Oxted on a crew training run, pending displacement of the Class 205 DMUs. Only the up line is now in use and the up bay track has been lifted. It is hoped that the station will not be demolished as in the future the down platform could be used by Spa Valley Railway passengers.

GROOMBRIDGE JUNCTION: With the junction in the background, Class 4MT No 80147 heads for Eridge and Eastbourne with the 12.39pm train from Tunbridge Wells West on 16 March 1958.

At the same location on 6 May 1988 there are no trains, but the track awaits renovation for eventual use by Spa Valley trains between Tunbridge Wells West and Eridge. (See also pages 94-97.)

Eastbourne to Groombridge

EASTBOURNE: Class 'E4' No 32470 stands at Eastbourne on the 1.11pm train to Hailsham with set No 609 on 13 April 1962. Most services ran through to Tunbridge Wells, but a small number of peak-period trains ran only between Eastbourne and Hailsham.

   The centre line has been removed, but little else has changed in the more recent photograph. Class 421 (4-CIG) No 1201 has just arrived forming the 13.53 service from Brighton on 1 August 1987.

HAMPDEN PARK: Trains crossing at Hampden Park on 14 August 1956 are, on the left, the 2.45pm to Tunbridge Wells West behind Standard 4MT No 80010, and on the right an electric train comprising two 2-NOL units, Nos 1813 and 1834, forming the 2.14pm service from Brighton to Ore.

Trains between Brighton and Hastings pass through Hampden Park twice within about 10 minutes, as they have to reverse at Eastbourne; the direct line bypassing Eastbourne was closed in January 1969. On 10 April 2003 Class 421 (3-COP) No 1401 forms the 08.33 Hastings to Brighton service.

POLEGATE (OLD) (I): Class 'U1' No 31892 enters the station with the 4.47pm Eastbourne to Hailsham train on 16 August 1962, a task more appropriate for a tank engine. The line continuing into the left background is the direct connection between Lewes and Hastings avoiding Eastbourne. This is the second Polegate station and was built on a new site in 1881 when the junction for Hailsham was changed from east-facing to west-facing.

All that remains of the direct line is seen in this photograph taken on 10 April 2003. Passing the same point as the steam engine above is Class 421 (4-CIG) No 1741 forming the 13.00 Hastings to Brighton service.

85

POLEGATE (OLD) (2): Class 'K' No 32348 stands at Polegate with the 5.34pm to Hailsham, a distance of only 3 miles.

Polegate station was rebuilt in 1986 on its original site, with the closure of the 1881 station, and this was all that remained of the latter on 1 August 1987. Even in 2003 the earthworks for the platforms can still be seen, although most of the platforms themselves have been removed.

POLEGATE (NEW): The 4.10pm from Tonbridge to Eastbourne joins the coast line at the west end of Polegate behind Class 4MT No 80016 on 29 March 1961.

The line from Hailsham followed the treeline on the right of the 'present' picture. On the left is the main line with Class 421 (4-CIG) No 1741 entering the new station on 10 April 2003.

HAILSHAM (1): BR Standard Class 4MT No 80140 heads the 6.00pm Eastbourne to Tunbridge Wells West train at Hailsham on 13 April 1962. Unlike many country stations, this was conveniently situated for the town.

A visit on 5 April 1986 found the station site under development. The key to matching the views is the white house on the extreme left. A third visit in 2003 found that the area in front of the houses was a rather untidy car park.

Opposite page **HAILSHAM (2): Another BR Standard 2-6-4T 4MT, No 80148, leaves with the 4.10pm Tonbridge to Eastbourne train on the same day. As mentioned opposite, there is now no trace of the station here, as seen on 1 July 2003, although the houses in the background in the top photograph still exist, now hidden by the newer houses.**

HELLINGLY station was photographed on 18 November 1961 with Class 4MT No 80137 on an Eastbourne to Tunbridge Wells train. A short branch line with its own platform ran from here to a psychiatric hospital, operated by a small electric locomotive drawing power from an overhead cable.

The second view shows the station on 27 April 1972, seven years after closure. It still exists today and is privately owned; as seen on 1 July 2003, it is well hidden behind trees, no doubt desirable for privacy as a public footpath now occupies the trackbed. *Edwin Wilmshurst/R. M. Casserley/TG*

WALDRON & HORAM ROAD was called Waldon & Horam (and various combinations) until September 1953, when it became Horam, the name retained until closure. A special train on the line on 22 March 1964 was hauled by 'Battle of Britain' Class No 34066 *Spitfire*; the station is in the background.

The trackbed is a continuation of the public footpath from Hailsham and Hellingly, but the view of the station site from this point is blocked by houses.

HEATHFIELD: The pick-up freight from Tunbridge Wells West is seen at Heathfield on 14 August 1956 with Class 'C' No 31588 in charge. There is a tunnel just out of sight at the far end of the platforms.

The once attractive station area has become an eyesore, with a scrapyard, car repairers and a recycling centre. The tunnel is visible between the line of vehicles on 1 July 2003.

ROTHERFIELD & MARK CROSS: On 25 January 1964 the 9.56am from Tonbridge to Eastbourne enters Rotherfield & Mark Cross behind Standard 4MT No 80144.

Following closure the station lay derelict for several years, as seen in the second photograph from 1970, before being bought as a private residence, seen in the third view on 1 May 1986. *Edwin Wilmshurst/TG (2)*

Groombridge to Three Bridges

GROOMBRIDGE station is seen first on 2 September 1961, looking towards Tunbridge Wells, with the goods shed in the background. The train is the 2.00pm from Tunbridge Wells West to Oxted, formed of Class 'H' No 31278 and set No 656, converted by the SR for push-pull working from pre-Grouping stock.

Even before closure the condition of the station had become poor and the canopies and some of the buildings dismantled. The second photograph shows the station on 1 May 1986, almost a year after closure.

The land was subsequently sold for redevelopment, but the station building was retained and is in use as offices. This necessitated a minor but irritating diversion of the line by the Spa Valley Railway, as seen on 5 June 2003.

London Brighton and South Coast Railway

———————

Partridge Green to

Groombridge

GROOMBRIDGE NEW STATION: Trains cross in the cutting between Groombridge station and Groombridge Junction on 2 May 1958. Approaching is Class 'U1' No 31910 on the 1.47pm Tunbridge Wells West to Victoria train, photographed from the 12.55pm from Brighton to Tonbridge, hauled by a Class 'L'.

A new station has been built in this cutting by the Spa Valley Railway; the old one can be seen beyond the road bridge in this summer 2003 photograph.

GROOMBRIDGE JUNCTION: On the approach to Groombridge station, with the signals for the Junction in the background, the line to Eridge curves to the left and that to the right is for Ashurst and East Grinstead. The train is the 10.45am from Eastbourne to Tunbridge Wells West hauled by 4MT No 80147 on 16 March 1958.

The junction is still intact, but the Ashurst line has been truncated and only continues for a few hundred yards beyond this point. The other line continues to Eridge, to which the Spa Valley Railway hopes to run services.

WITHYAM: The section between Ashurst Junction and East Grinstead was single track. Class 4MT No 42106 is pictured at Withyam with the 10.08am Victoria to Tunbridge Wells West train on 2 May 1958. Although built to a design by Stanier and numbered in the Midland Region series, these engines were not far from home as they were built at Brighton in 1950.

The station building is now a private house and the trackbed a public footpath. Part of the platform can be seen in the undergrowth on this wet morning at the end of June 2003.

HARTFIELD: BR Standard 4MT No 80095 runs into Hartfield with the 5.47pm Tunbridge Wells West to Victoria train, with set No 194 leading. Since closure of the line the station has been beautifully restored and in June 2003 was being used by a children's playgroup.

FOREST ROW: Heading for the Eastbourne line via Ashurst and Birchden Junctions on 22 March 1964 is a special train hauled by Class 'Q1' No 33027. On the left is a DMU of Class 3D (later 207), No 1303, forming a Tunbridge Wells to East Grinstead service.

In contrast to Hartfield, Forest Row station has been demolished and the site given over to various uses including a fire station, health club and veterinary surgery. Behind the wall is a recycling centre and to the right is a Scout hut, as seen on 30 June 2003.

EAST GRINSTEAD HIGH LEVEL: On 27 July 1955 Class 'D3' No 32390, the last of its class and only a matter of weeks before withdrawal, is ready to depart on a train to Three Bridges. The High Level station crossed the Low Level one at right angles.

Once the High Level station closed the rail overbridge was removed, so standing at the same position today reveals the Low Level platforms, while the High Level station site has become a car park.

GRANGE ROAD: A freight train approaches Grange Road for Three Bridges on 3 June 1960, hauled by Class 'C2X' No 32527. In the ensuing four decades the area around the station has been transformed with new shops, houses and roads. As best as can be judged, this is the same location on 10 April 1992.

Eastbourne to Hastings

PEVENSEY & WESTHAM: The 2.50pm Eastbourne to Bexhill train enters Pevensey & Westham station on 7 October 1933. The engine is Class 'D1' No 2254.

This is still a pleasant station, complete with signal box and main building, and despite the current policy of having short station names, it has retained its double name. On 8 April 2003 the 10.47 Victoria to Hastings service is formed of Class 421 (4-CIG) No 1741. *H. C. Casserley/TG*

NORMANS BAY HALT: The desolate-looking halt is close to the beach and popular in summer. These two views, looking towards Bexhill, date from 22 October 1934 and 8 April 2003, between which dates the halt has been rebuilt and hedges on both sides of the line have narrowed the field of vision. However, the white buildings in the distance are still visible, although the crossing keeper's house has been demolished. The approaching train made an unscheduled stop here, as this station has only an hourly service for much of the day and the previous train had been cancelled. *H. C. Casserley/TG*

COLLINGTON HALT opened in 1905, closed a year later, then re-opened in 1911 as West Bexhill Halt. It was renamed Collington Halt in 1929. SR-built electric units of Class 4-LAV Nos 2950 and 2953 pass through the Halt forming a Victoria to Ore service on 14 August 1956.

On 10 April 2003 Class 421 (4-CIG) No 1874 enters Collington as the 08.20 West Worthing to Hastings service. The footbridge, sloped rather than stepped, is a public right of way and was installed by the SR following electrification to replace a boarded crossing. Both platforms are now of concrete construction.

ST LEONARDS WEST MARINA: On 23 October 1934 the 10.00am Eastbourne to Rye train is at St Leonards West Marina behind Class 'D3' No 2374. To the right of the station is the motive power depot.

West Marina is the first of four stations within 2 miles, so it is no surprise that not all could survive into the 21st century. The second photograph shows West Marina on 8 May 1977, 10 years after closure; the westbound platform has been removed. The motive power depot closed in 1958 and a new depot built for DMUs nearer to Hastings.

The eastbound platform still exists, as seen on 25 April 2003. Class 421 (4-CIG) No 1744 forms the 10.44 Hastings to Brighton service, while the old engine shed area is used for berthing EMUs, in this instance Class 421 No 1843. *H. C. Casserley (2)/TG*

Hastings toward Ashford

HASTINGS (1): Class 'H' No 31520 approaches Hastings with the 2.53pm train from Ashford on 3 June 1958.

The line was dieselised in 1962 and on 5 April 1986 DMU Class 3H No 1102 (later Class 205 No 205002) forms the 15.30 service from Ashford into Hastings. These units continued to work this service until May 2004. Three evening trains continue to Eastbourne and three morning trains start from Eastbourne. The semaphore signals were still in use in 2004.

HASTINGS (2): Class 3H No 1102 stands in the bay platform waiting to leave as the 16.42 all-stations service to Ashford on 5 April 1986. By this time one of the three halts on the line, Snaleham, had been closed.

A visit in April 2003 found the same units at work, with Class 205 No 205028 forming the 10.34 to Ashford. Shortage of units during this month resulted in many cancellations and the provision of substitute buses.

ORE: Electric units of Class 2-NOL, Nos 1826 and 1846, form the 2.42pm service to Brighton on 3 June 1958. Ore was (and still is) the furthest point east on the electrified part of the coast line.

There was an electric depot at Ore, so most train services began or terminated here. This is no longer the case as the depot has been demolished, and very few EMUs run east of Hastings. The station buildings have also been demolished, and the high fencing gives an indication of the vandalism from which the station suffers; new waiting shelters were severely damaged within hours of being erected. On 20 May 2004 Class 207 No 207202 works the only fast train to Ashford, calling only at Ore and Rye. From the introduction of the new timetable three days later, all Hastings-Ashford trains were scheduled to be operated by new Class 170 DMUs.

THREE OAKS & GUESTLING HALT: The line was double track between Hastings and Ashford, so even the halts had two platforms. This is the Hastings-bound platform of Three Oaks & Guestling Halt in 1970.

Now called simply Three Oaks, this is the station on 8 May 1990, with Class 207 No 207011 leaving as the 17.06 service to Ashford. Note the several passengers ascending the steps from the platform. The track has been singled and all trains now use the Hastings-bound platform.

DOLEHAM HALT was photographed looking toward Ashford in 1970. The Hastings-bound platform is still wooden, but the Ashford side has been refurbished.

It was the Ashford side that was retained when the line was singled in 1979. On 8 May 1990 Class 205 No 205009 approaches Doleham forming the 16.11 Ashford to Hastings service.

WINCHELSEA is an isolated station three-quarters of a mile from the town along a narrow winding road, followed by a very steep climb on a main road. This is the Ashford-bound platform in 1970, when the station still had oil lamps.

The Ashford platform has been refurbished, but the Hastings platform has been removed. The main station building is a private house. On 1 July 2003 the 13.52 service from Ashford is formed of Class 205 No 205025.

RYE: On 8 August 1989 two DMUs cross at Rye: on the left is Class 207 No 207004 forming the 15.13 from Hastings, and on the right Class 205 No 205018 as the 15.11 from Ashford.

The main station building and signal box are still in use. In anticipation of the withdrawal of all Class 205/207 units, on 20 May 2004 two round trips were in the hands of a Class 170 DMU. No 170726, forming an Ashford-Hastings service, waits at Rye to pass an Ashford-bound train.

Hastings towards Tunbridge Wells

HASTINGS (3): Class 'D1' No 31246 brings the stock of the 11.35am to Ashford into Hastings on 3 June 1958.

On 5 April 1986, the date of the second photograph, Class 201 (6S) No 1005 arrives at its destination forming the 09.15 service from Charing Cross. These DMUs, built at Eastleigh and starting work in 1957, were built to a narrow loading gauge especially for the London to Hastings line; they were displaced by EMUs in 1986. Several of these vehicles still exist and have been reformed into unit No 1001; for a short period in 2002 it was used on Charing Cross to Hastings services, due to a shortage of EMUs.

With not many more months before withdrawal, Class 421 (4-CIG) 'slam door' unit No 1809 forms the 08.15 from Charing Cross on 25 April 2003.

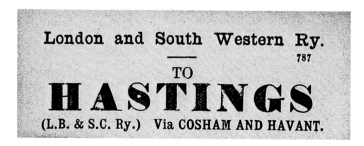

CROWHURST (1): 'Schools' Class locomotives were used on many of the expresses between London and Hastings, and here No 30926 *Repton* brings the 10.10am train from Hastings to Charing Cross into Crowhurst on 3 June 1958. Crowhurst was the junction station for the Bexhill West line, and there were bays on both the up and down side for the branch trains.

New units of Class 375 began to take over from Mark I 'slam door' units in early 2003. On 25 April Class 375 No 375708 leaves Crowhurst as the 12.35 service from Charing Cross to Hastings.

BEXHILL WEST: A special train from Paddington traversed the branch on 19 October 1958. This is the return working shortly before departure, hauled by Class 'E1' No 31019. By this time, all local trains were operated by DMUs.

The station building has been beautifully renovated and is used as an auction house. Much of the yard is an industrial estate, but it was possible to get a glimpse of the station clock on 10 April 2003.

Kent & East Sussex line

BODIAM: Three stages in the life of a station – on 14 September 1957 a hop pickers' empty stock working stands at Bodiam behind Class 'A1X' No 32678.

By 1987 a completely overgrown area engulfs the station, but still a tiny sign of life in seen in the form of the steam engine in the yard.

The present-day station reflects its past glory and indeed more, now that it is the western terminus of the KESR. *Edwin Wilmshurst/TG (2)*

NORTHIAM station is deserted on 19 August 1933, but a train was expected later in the day. There were four trains on weekdays, with a fifth train on Wednesdays and Saturdays.

The imminent arrival of a train on 5 June 1996 is greeted by an encouraging number of passengers waiting for the return to Tenterden. There are currently five trains on the standard timetable. *H. C. Casserley/TG*

First Class
A supplementary fare is payable for travel in this coach. 30p per person, per single journey Pay on the train Treat yourself and travel in style!

INDEX OF LOCATIONS